An AI Guide for CPAs

Updated for 2026

TAX
DIRECTOR
SERVICES

AN AI GUIDE FOR CPAs
Copyright © 2025–2026 Tax Director Services, Inc. All rights reserved.

ISBN: 979-8-9868657-3-7

For information, contact:
Tax Director Services, Inc.
1273 Horsham Way
Apex, NC 27502

www.nctaxdirector.com

Table of Contents

1 Preliminary Matters

1.1 About the author

Trent Green is an author, CPE developer and instructor, conference speaker, and Fortune 500 corporate-tax consultant through his firm, Tax Director Services (nctaxdirector.com). Before founding TDS he served as:

- Head of Tax, PROS Holdings – $160 million public software company
- Tax Director, PwC
- Head of International Tax, SAS – $2.7 billion multinational in 50+ countries

Trent began his career with Coopers & Lybrand (now PwC). He holds a B.A. with a Business minor and a Master of Accounting degree from UNC–Chapel Hill. A CPE instructor and conference presenter since 2009, he earned the NCACPA 5.0 Speaker Award in 2016.

Trent engages in community service, has coached baseball, and is an active member of The Church of Jesus Christ of Latter-day Saints. He lives with his family in Apex, North Carolina.

1.2 Other books and CPE courses by the author

- The Missing Tax Accounting Guide: A Plain-English Introduction to ASC 740
- Alteryx for Accounting, Tax, and Finance Professionals
- Tax Department Productivity: People, Processes, and Technology
- The Step-by-Step Guide to Starting and Running a Small Business

1.3 Website and LinkedIn Profile

- Website — For CPE and consulting details, visit www.nctaxdirector.com.
- LinkedIn — Accounting, tax, and finance professionals can connect with me at linkedin.com/in/trentgreen.

2 Getting Started with AI Using ChatGPT

2.1 The goal of this guide

The goal of this guide is to help CPAs become proficient in the AI tools, technologies, and techniques that matter in our profession, with a minimal investment of time.

2.2 Using AI significantly improves professional performance

Consider results from a 2023 MIT experiment that compared professionals who used ChatGPT on writing tasks with a control group that did not:

- 40 % faster task-completion time[1]
- 18 % higher independent-quality scores[2]
- Performance gap narrowed—lower-skill participants' output rose to near higher-skill levels[3]
- Job-satisfaction boost: ≈ 0.5 standard-deviation increase[4]

In summary, using AI tools effectively will demonstrably increase your productivity.

2.3 Use ChatGPT unless there is a compelling reason to use another platform

- In November 2022, ChatGPT became the first AI chatbot released to the general public and has steadily gained momentum ever since.

- Just because ChatGPT was released first doesn't mean it will remain the dominant AI platform in the future any more than Yahoo retained its lead over Google in search.

---

[1] Source: Noy & Zhang, "Experimental Evidence on the Productivity Effects of Generative AI," Science, 14 July 2023.

[2] Id.

[3] MIT News summary – https://news.mit.edu/2023/study-finds-chatgpt-boosts-worker-productivity-writing-0714

[4] Id.

- That said, until and unless there is a clear and compelling reason to change, I recommend that CPAs focus on developing proficiency with ChatGPT rather than divide their attention between multiple AI platforms.

Alternatives to ChatGPT

Throughout this material, I have placed an emphasis on ChatGPT. However, the same principles apply to using competing AI models such as:

- Gemini (Google)
- Perplexity AI
- Llama (Meta)
- Claude (Anthropic)
- Copilot (Microsoft)

Based on the principles of productivity (which includes continuity and efficiency), I will continue to use ChatGPT as my go-to AI platform until another one clearly separates itself from the pack.

Don't get hung up on which model is "the best"

What if you personally prefer an AI platform other than ChatGPT? Here's my take:

- ChatGPT, Claude, Perplexity – the is like comparing one car model to another
- Your skill in working with AI is far more important than which platform you use (ChatGPT, etc.).
- Whatever AI platform you settle on, learn it deeply and build repeatable procedures.

Key takeaway: The AI platform you settle on is less important than you adopt, use, and master an AI planform.

2.4   Focus on one AI platform—Not on chasing the "best" one

The professional environment and AI platform choices

This guide focuses on ChatGPT, but it's important to acknowledge reality:

- Some professionals are required to use a specific platform based on workplace policy (for example, Microsoft Copilot).
- Others may simply prefer a different AI platform.

That's fine. Either way, the core principles in this book still apply.

Why I focus on ChatGPT

- ChatGPT gained a tremendous first-mover advantage when in launched in November 2022 when it became the first AI platform released to the general public and has steadily gained momentum since then.

- I adopted ChatGPT from the outset, and until there is a clear and compelling reason to change, I'm going to stay with it.

- Regardless of the platform you choose, my strong recommendation is that you focus on developing deep proficiency with one AI tool rather than dividing your attention across many platforms.

Alternatives to ChatGPT

As I noted previously, the overarching principles, methods, and techniques in this book apply to other AI platforms aside from ChatGPT, including:

- Copilot (Microsoft)
- Gemini (Google)
- Claude (Anthropic)
- Perplexity
- Llama (Meta)

The platform matters less than how you use it

Don't get hung up on which platform is "best"

If you step back, comparing AI platforms today is a lot like comparing car models. Each has strengths and weaknesses, but none of them matter much if you don't know how to drive well.

In summary, adopting an AI platform and mastering how to use it matters far more than which platform you adopt. The real advantage comes from consistent use, thoughtful prompting, and integrating AI into how you actually work.

2.5   ChatGPT and other AI terms defined

ChatGPT – A chatbot developed by OpenAI that answers questions, analyzes data, and generates text-based output.

GPT – Short for Generative Pre-trained Transformer, the language-model architecture that powers ChatGPT.

Large Language Model (LLM) – A class of AI models trained on vast amounts of text to learn statistical patterns in language and generate human-like responses.
- GPT-4 and GPT-5.2 are examples of LLMs.

Generative AI – A broad term for AI tools that create new content rather than simply retrieving existing information. Examples include:
- ChatGPT → Text
- DALL·E → Images
- Sora → Video

Prompt – The text, question, instructions, or files you provide to an LLM.

Hallucination – A confident-sounding but factually incorrect response generated by an LLM.
- CPAs should always verify AI output before relying on it.
- This is not new; we have also been trained not to blindly rely on traditional Google search results.

2.6 Signing Up for ChatGPT

Sign-up steps

1) Visit https://chat.openai.com.

2) Click *Sign up* and follow the prompts.

3) Pick the plan that fits your situation:
   a. Free
   b. ChatGPT Plus – $20/month for one seat
   c. ChatGPT Team – $30 per user per month with a two-seat minimum
   d. ChatGPT Enterprise – custom pricing, 150-seat minimum

Selecting the Best Plan for CPAs

- Just experimenting → Start on the Free tier, but expect to hit model and rate limits quickly.

- Solo or boutique CPAs → ChatGPT Team (not Plus). As noted above, there's a two-seat minimum, but this plan unlocks:
  o Access to the newest LLMs (larger context windows, stronger reasoning).
  o Deep web search with clickable citations—incredibly powerful for research
  o Advanced Data Analysis
  o Higher message caps and faster response times than the Free and Plus tiers.
  o An admin console to invite or remove others from your plan as needed.

- Firm or corporate employees → You'll have access to an Enterprise version (of ChatGPT or some other platform).

In summary, the free tier beats no AI at all, but ChatGPT Team delivers the most value for CPAs who pay their own way. The rest of this guide assumes you have a Team subscription.

A Note on Privacy and Confidentiality

- Data privacy is important for CPAs handling sensitive company and client information.

- One of the key advantages of the Team plan is that your inputs are *not* used to train OpenAI's models.

- The Team plan also includes enterprise-grade encryption and privacy protections—critical for meeting internal control, regulatory, and ethical obligations.

To sum up in OpenAI's own words:

"Your data remains private and secure. Nothing entered into ChatGPT Team is used to train AI models, and OpenAI cannot access or use your data unless you explicitly request technical support."[5]

2.7 The ChatGPT interface

Once you log in to ChatGPT, the interface looks something like the illustration that follows (I say "something" because the format periodically changes):

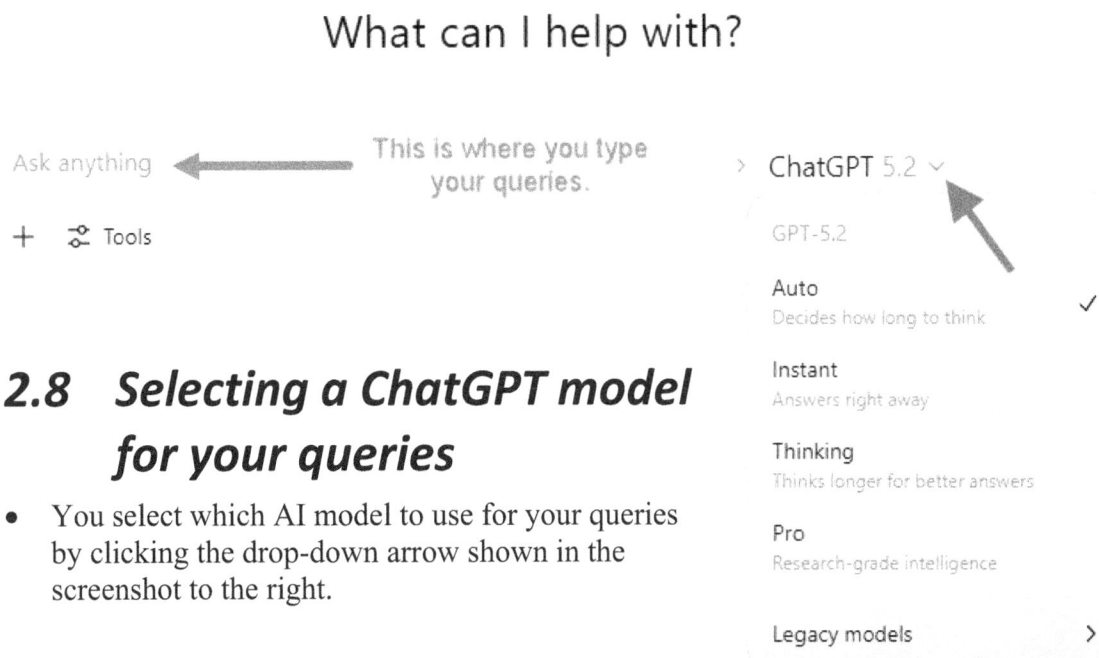

What can I help with?

Ask anything ⟵ This is where you type your queries.

+ ⇄ Tools

> ChatGPT 5.2 ⌄

GPT-5.2

Auto ✓
Decides how long to think

Instant
Answers right away

Thinking
Thinks longer for better answers

Pro
Research-grade intelligence

Legacy models >

2.8 Selecting a ChatGPT model for your queries

- You select which AI model to use for your queries by clicking the drop-down arrow shown in the screenshot to the right.

---

[5] Additional information can be found here: https://openai.com/chatgpt/privacy.

- Later on, I'll cover in detail which model to select for your queries and why.

- For now, we'll assume you are using the default GPT-5.2 model for your queries.

2.9 ChatGPT's interface changes, but the basics don't

- For context, Google's user interface ("UI") hasn't changed much in nearly three decades.

- ChatGPT's UI has been more dynamic, but the core experience—typing into a familiar "Ask anything" bar—remains intuitive for anyone who's used a search engine.

- That said, ChatGPT's home screen isn't as minimalistic as Google's; there's more going on.

- This reflects a positive trend: the platform keeps evolving: OpenAI regularly adds features, reorganizes menus, and refines the layout accordingly.

- The tradeoff is that there's more to learn and more to keep up with.

- But even as the UI shifts, the basics remain the same. So if something in this book looks slightly different down the road, don't worry—if you understand the core principles, you'll still be able to figure things out.

2.10 A quick review before moving on

To sum up where we are so far:

- You now understand key AI terminology.
- You've signed up for ChatGPT's "Team" plan (or you have access to another AI platform) and
- You've logged into ChatGPT.

If you've gotten this far, you're ready to start using ChatGPT to solve real problems and accelerate your performance!

3 Prompt Engineering Basics

Google is a <u>search</u> engine; ChatGPT is an <u>answer</u> engine.

You've come this far and the "Ask anything" bar is staring at you.
So, what you do type? That's what "prompt engineering" is all about. Ask anything

3.1 What is prompt engineering?

- Prompt engineering is more than just typing something into the prompt box. It's the practice of communicating with a generative AI platform like ChatGPT in a thoughtful, systematic way to get better results.

- Prompt engineering is part art and part science. It's about crafting the wording of AI queries to get relevant, high-quality, and accurate responses from ChatGPT.

- If you're used to traditional search engines like Google, think of prompt engineering as the skill of creating good search terms – but on steroids!

3.2 Why prompt engineering is important

- If you type a question into ChatGPT without any context, you may get an inaccurate, confusing, or useless response.

- For example, let's say you're interested in international tax strategies and you start with the query: "What is a Dutch sandwich?"

- With no context, ChatGPT might return an answer like: "A 'Broodje kroket' is a type of sandwich made with a deep-fried beef croquette on a bun with mustard."

- This is why prompt engineering matters—it helps ChatGPT generate responses that are relevant, useful, accurate, and tailored to your needs.

3.3 Setting ChatGPT's expertise (CPA-specific)

Getting started

- Prompt engineering can be extremely detailed and elaborate, but it doesn't have to be for most queries.

- The purpose of prompt engineering is to set ChatGPT's area of focus, identity, or domain expertise.

- So, as noted earlier, instead of jumping straight to your question, begin with a prompt like:
  - o You are an expert in US GAAP.
  - o You are a corporate tax expert.
  - o You are an Excel expert.

A CPA-related example

TR   You are a US corporate tax expert

(logo)   Hello! As an AI language model, I can provide information on US corporate tax rules and regulations. However, I cannot provide legal or financial advice, and I always recommend consulting with a licensed tax professional for any specific questions or concerns related to corporate taxes. How can I assist you today?

Key point: Once you set ChatGPT's identity and expertise, you can ask follow-up questions on the same subject in a natural, conversational manner.

3.4   Prompt engineering methods, strategies and approaches

You can apply the following prompt engineering methods across a wide range of personal and professional contexts.

ROLE - Assign a Role

Following the "You are a corporate tax expert" example above, you can ask ChatGPT to take on practically any role:

- Act as a [name the role] expert.
- You are a [name the role].

TASK – Create or assign a task

- Your task is to [name the task].
- Design a [name the task].
- Create a [name the task].
- You must [explain the task].
- Extract data from [a PDF, image, etc.].

BACKGROUND/CONTEXT

- Assume that [provide details].
- The situation is [description].
- I am [describe your present state].

FORMAT – Describe the form of the output

- Provide a list of bullet points that [provide a description].
- Provide a step-by-step process for [provide a description].
- List the output in a table with [describe the table format].

SIMPLIFY – Simplify or break down complex topics

- Break down [technical accounting or tax topic] into simpler terms.
- Use an example to explain [describe the subject matter].
- Use an analogy to explain [describe the concept].

GOAL – Clarify goals, objectives, and outcomes

- Your goal is to [describe the goal].
- Your objective is to [describe the objective].
- The purpose of this analysis is to [describe the purpose].
- Some examples of what I am looking for are [list sample responses].
- You can also use the following prompt:
  - Ask me questions if anything is unclear or if you need more information that will measurably improve the results.

PARAMETERS – Provide boundaries and limitations

- Only consider [the desired limitations].
- Any recommendations should be at least [provide the parameters].
- Output should include only [list the constraints].

Other prompt engineering guidance

Here is some other prompt engineering guidance:

- ChatGPT is more effective when you tell it what to do ("do") rather than what not to do ("don't").[6]
- You don't need to be polite ("Please," etc.).
- Use line breaks to separate concepts, instructions, or questions:
  - This is done by pressing SHIFT+ENTER.

---

[6] You will generally get better results if you affirmatively state what you want (The output should include only…) vs. what you don't want ("The output should exclude anything that…"). In short, positive instructions provide the AI model with a clear target to hit.

o   Note: If you press only ENTER, you'll immediately submit your prompt.

- Instruct the model to ask you follow-up questions if needed to improve the response.
- Be wordy in your descriptions. You're not aiming for perfect grammar—you're aiming to be as descriptive as possible to get better answers from the model.

For example, when assigning ChatGPT a role:

- Good: Act as an accounting expert.
- Better: Act as a US GAAP expert.
- Best: Act as a US GAAP accounting expert.

From a grammar standpoint, "accounting" is redundant in the "Best" example. But from a prompt engineering perspective, including "accounting" gives ChatGPT one more signal that helps it generate more relevant, focused responses.

3.5   Prompt engineering in a process, not a one-shot prompt

Prompt engineering isn't just about the first question you ask—it includes everything that follows. The most useful responses often come *after* your initial query, once you clarify, reframe, or ask for a different format.

Here are follow-up prompts that work especially well for CPAs:

- "Break this down by step for a [CFP, client, etc.] explanation?"
- "Summarize this in bullet points I can paste into an email."
- "Rephrase this using plain language for a non-technical audience."
- "Give me a numeric example using simple, round numbers."
- "Format this as a table that I can copy into Excel."
- "Compare these two positions side by side (e.g., IFRS vs. GAAP)."
- "Add citations to [ASC sections, the Internal Revenue Code, etc.]."
- "List possible objections or risks related to this approach."

The idea is simple: you can continue to shape ChatGPT's output just like you would in a back-and-forth conversation—and often, the best material comes two or three prompts in.

Also, don't overthink it. A lot of social media posts—especially on LinkedIn—make prompt engineering look like an overly complex, formulaic, one-shot magic trick. They give the impression that unless you craft the perfect, expert-level prompt up front, you'll either get something useless in return or somehow break the system. That's not how it works.

Even for tasks of medium complexity, it's rare to get everything you want the way you want it in one try. Think of prompt engineering as an iterative process—you're shaping and refining the output until it gives you what you need. Adopting this mindset can help you relax, dive in, and start using ChatGPT *now*. Over time, you'll get better, faster, and more confident just by doing it.

3.6 A YouTube overview of prompt engineering

Here's a short video that covers many of the concepts in this chapter:

- Go to nctaxdirector.com/library
- Scroll to the section titled "Artificial Intelligence for CPAs"
- Click on the video: "An Introduction to ChatGPT Prompt Engineering for CPAs"

Artificial Intelligence for CPAs ∧

Download the PDF: An AI Guide for CPAs (2024)

Watch the video: An Introduction to ChatGPT Prompt Engineering for CPAs (1:48)

Watch the video: Prompt Engineering for Tax Questions (1:36)

Watch the video: Prompt Engineering for Federal Tax Updates (1:33)

Watch the video: Prompt Engineering and State and Local Tax (SALT) Updates (0:59)

Watch the video: Prompt Engineering for Accounting Questions (0:46)

Watch the video: Prompt Engineering for Audit and Accounting Updates (1:01)

Watch the video: ChatGPT Output Cautions and Limitations (2:34)

4 Selecting the Right LLM Model for Your Queries

4.1 Where we are and what's next

In the first three chapters, you:

- Learned key AI terminology
- Signed up for the ChatGPT Team plan
- Became familiar with ChatGPT's user interface, and
- Practiced prompt engineering (e.g., "Act as an accounting expert")

With that foundation, you're now ready to learn how to choose the right language model (LLM) for your queries. This chapter will explain:

- How the models differ
- When to switch between them, and
- How to manage usage so you get the best mix of speed and quality.

4.2 An introduction to ChatGPT's LLC models

Every time you start a new thread in ChatGPT, the system defaults to a general-purpose LLM. Most of the time, that's perfectly fine. However, it's not your only option.

ChatGPT offers multiple language models that differ in speed, depth of reasoning, and cost. Because the names and labels of these models change over time, I'm going to use a more stable convention for LLMs throughout this book:

- Regular
- Medium
- Advanced

As of this writing, those tiers generally map as follows:

- Regular – ChatGPT 5.2, which is fast and well-suited for most everyday professional tasks.
- Medium – This is the "Thinking" model, which take more time to reason through complex or ambiguous inputs.

ChatGPT 5.2 ⌄

GPT-5.2

Auto
Decides how long to think

Instant
Answers right away

Thinking
Thinks longer for better answers

Pro
Research-grade intelligence

Legacy models

- Advanced – This is the "Pro" model, which is designed for the most demanding technical work where accuracy and depth matter more than speed.
- As a CPA, I find no use for the "Instant" or "Legacy" models.

The specific model names may change, but the conceptual distinction between regular, medium, and advanced reasoning models is much more stable. That's why I'll refer to models using this framework going forward.

On the Team plan, you can switch between these models using the drop-down menu at the top of the chat window. The model you select applies to all queries in that thread unless you change it.

The key takeaway is simple: different models are optimized for different types of work, and choosing the right level of reasoning can materially improve both the speed and quality of your output.

4.3   The car analogy for picking a model

You don't need to get hung up on trying to pick the "perfect" model for every query. To make it easier, think of ChatGPT models like cars:

- Driving any car beats walking—by a long shot.
- Thus, just by using ChatGPT (vs. a traditional search engine), you're already way ahead of the game.

That said, some cars are better suited for specific tasks:

- A 4WD for snow and rough terrain
- A compact for city traffic and tight parking
- A truck for hauling
- A sedan for long highway trips

It's the same with ChatGPT models. The goal is to pick the one that's the best match for this task you're working on.

4.4   How CPAs Should Use Regular, Medium, and Advanced Models

- Once you understand that different models (or LLMs) are optimized for different types of work, the next question is how to use them effectively in practice.
- Some CPA tasks and projects are routine and well-scoped. Others are judgment-heavy, technically complex, or messy.

- The value of choosing between regular, medium, and advanced models comes from matching the level of reasoning to the nature of the task at hand.

Regular models: your default

For most day-to-day CPA work, the regular model should be your starting point. This includes tasks such as:

- Drafting and editing emails and routine correspondence
- Summarizing articles, guidance, or documents
- Answering straightforward accounting or tax questions
- Working with spreadsheets when the logic is clean and structured

Regular models are fast, responsive, and more than capable when your prompt is clear. In practice, you'll find they can handle a large portion of your work without any need to switch.

Medium models: when the problem needs more thought

The medium model is useful when the task requires more deliberate reasoning but doesn't rise to the level of a full technical deep dive. This is often the case when:

- The facts are incomplete, disorganized, or evolving.
- You're exploring alternatives or tradeoffs.
- You're framing a complex issue before moving into detailed analysis.

Medium models take longer to respond, but they're better at staying focused and avoiding shallow answers.

Advanced models: save these for when it really matters

The advanced model is designed for situations where accuracy and depth matter more than speed. Typical use cases include:

- Advanced memos requiring detailed citations.
- Analyzing dense PDFs, contracts, or technical guidance
- Reviewing complex workpapers or supporting documentation.
- Projects where you're synthesizing data from many sources.
- Any other situations where you want the model to reason carefully and explicitly

Advanced models are slower and may be subject, usage limits, and token costs. Because of that, they're best reserved for high-value work where the incremental improvement in reasoning quality justifies the additional time or cost.

A practical selection approach that works well for CPAs

In many cases, the most effective approach is not to pick a single model and stick with it. Instead:

- Start with the regular model to frame the issue and provide the data and inputs needed for the analysis.
- Switch to the medium or advanced model to do the analysis and to provide the initial output.
- Switch back to a regular model for follow-up questions, drafting, formatting, or additional analysis.

This lets you combine the strengths of each model in a way that balances speed, accuracy, and cost-effectiveness (if there is a token cost).

4.5   Managing usage and tokay capacity

How I think about usage

The rules around token usage and limits change over time, but I don't worry about every little adjustment. In practice, when I follow the model-selection approach outlined above, I rarely run into credit limitations.

As of this writing, I have only hit token limits once in the past several months in the course of normal CPA-related work using the medium and advanced models. Because of that:

- I don't hesitate to use the model (including the advanced mode) that I judge the best suited for the task I'm working on.
- I especially don't hold back when working on complex, technical, high-value deliverables.

If usage ever becomes a constraint, I deal with it then rather than letting it dictate how I work day to day.

How to check your usage

- If you want to review your usage, you can do so by navigating to:

  Workspace Settings → Billing → Token Usage

- This gives you visibility into how many tokens you've used and how that usage is trending during the current period.
- You can always purchase more tokens during the month if usage spikes unexpectedly.
- Your standard allocation resets the following month, so occasional higher usage doesn't permanently change your ChatGPT cost structure.

Key takeaway

Don't let token usage drive your behavior. Focus on getting the work done correctly and efficiently. Monitor usage when it matters, adjust when necessary, and move on.

5 Use ChatGPT to Get Accounting and Tax Answers

Now that you've learned the fundamentals of prompt engineering and the differences between regular, medium, and advanced LLMs, you're ready to see how ChatGPT can be used to answer real-world tax, accounting, and finance questions. YouTube videos for all of the examples that follow are available on my website:

- Go to www.nctaxdirector.com/library
- Click on the section "Artificial Intelligence for CPAs."

I recommend experimenting with the prompts as you go through each of the following examples because that will help build confidence and reinforce what you've learned.[7]

5.1 Sample tax question

The following is an example of how to use prompt engineering for tax questions.

Overview

- Opening prompt: You are a US corporate tax expert.
- Follow-up questions:
    - ☐ What is springing debt?
    - What does this have to do with Section 357?
    - Give me a numerical example of how the rules work.

YouTube example

Prompt Engineering for Tax Questions (1:36)

5.2 Sample accounting question

The following is an example of how to use prompt engineering for accounting questions.

Overview

- Opening prompt: You are a US GAAP accounting expert.
- Follow-up questions:
    - How is treasury stock created, and what's the accounting entry?
    - What is the entry to retire treasury stock?

---

[7] While the videos are slightly dated, they still demonstrate all of the core principles covered in this chapter.

YouTube example

Prompt Engineering for Accounting Questions (0:46)

5.3 Federal tax updates

The challenge of keeping current with tax laws

- Keeping up with tax laws can be challenging for CPAs, given the numerous types and the various jurisdictions they cover in the U.S. and globally.
- Reading or listening to tax updates can be inefficient, tedious, and time-consuming—especially when many rule changes don't apply to your industry, geography, or area of expertise.
- ChatGPT can streamline this process by customizing responses to your specific needs and preferences.

Using ChatGPT for federal tax updates

- Start with this prompt: You are a US corporate tax expert.
- Then follow up with questions like:
  - What are the 10 most impactful tax changes included in the One Big Beautiful Bill?
  - Which of those changes matter most if my company only has U.S. operations (and no international footprint)?
  - What are the 5 most significant tax provisions enacted after the TCJA but before the One Big Beautiful Bill?
  - Refine the list, taking into account that my company is a manufacturer based in the southeastern United States.

YouTube example

Prompt Engineering for Federal Tax Updates (1:33)

5.4 State tax ("SALT") updates

Overview

- With 50 states and roughly 12,000 sales tax jurisdictions, keeping up with state and local tax changes is no small task. ChatGPT can help you stay current through targeted, customized inquiries.
- As with federal tax updates, start with a prompt tailored to your location or filing footprint.
- For example: You are a North Carolina tax expert.
- Follow up with questions like:
  - What significant state-wide sales tax changes have been enacted since January 2020?

o   Were there any sales tax changes for Wake County?

YouTube example

Prompt Engineering and State and Local Tax (SALT) Updates (0:59)

5.5   Audit and accounting updates

Overview

- Audit and accounting updates are often important to CPAs—but like tax updates, they can be tedious to follow, especially when much of the information doesn't apply to your industry or area of expertise.
- To get a quick summary tailored to your needs, start with this prompt: You are a US GAAP accounting expert.
- Then follow up with questions like:
  o   What are the 10 most impactful accounting rule changes since 2018?
  o   List only changes that relate to revenue recognition.
  o   List the revenue recognition changes most relevant to pharmaceutical companies.

YouTube example

Prompt Engineering for Audit and Accounting Updates (1:01)

5.6   Observations on the Limitations of ChatGPT Output

Overview

While ChatGPT is a powerful tool, it's far from perfect. For example:

- Responses can sometimes be inconsistent.
- Sources are often not referenced—unless you specifically ask for them.
- The model can state things as fact with sufficient support to do so.

Despite these limitations, ChatGPT remains an extremely valuable tool in the hands of a skilled CPA. As always, use good judgment, verify your facts, and treat the model as a powerful assistant—not a final authority.

YouTube video

For additional thoughts on when to rely on ChatGPT (and when not to), see this video:

- ChatGPT Output Cautions and Limitations (2:34)

6 Advanced Prompting for CPA Projects

In Chapter 5, you saw that you can get a lot of value out of ChatGPT with simple, natural prompts, especially when your question is clear and the task is well-scoped. This chapter is for the situations where that approach starts to break down because you're dealing with more case-specific or advanced issues. The prompts that follow are templates you can reuse. Use them as-is, adjust them to fit your style.

6.1 PDF long document review

When reviewing long PDFs—whether they're tax memos, 10-Ks, audit reports, or technical guidance—ChatGPT can help you cut through the noise and surface what matters. The key is to guide the model to work in a structured, methodical way. Here's the prompt:

> You're reviewing a long technical document related to [topic]. Your goal is to identify key sections, summarize the main takeaways, and flag any inconsistencies or missing expected sections.
>
> First, identify and list the key structural sections. Then summarize each one clearly. Highlight red flags like incomplete tables, missing reconciliations, or unexplained changes.

6.2 Spreadsheet Analysis: Messy or Corrupted Data

When you're working with malformed or inconsistent spreadsheets—especially ones exported from legacy systems or poorly structured templates—ChatGPT can help restore order. The key is to prompt it to reason through the issues like a forensic accountant would.

> You're reviewing a spreadsheet with malformed or inconsistent data. Use reasoning to infer what the data should be based on surrounding context, column patterns, or accounting logic. Your tasks are to:
>
> 1) Identify rows or cells with probable corruption or misalignment.
> 2) Infer the correct value or format, and state your reasoning.
> 3) Output a cleaned version of the data in table format.
>
> Think step by step. Treat this as a forensic cleanup.

6.3 Tax Memo or Technical Writing

When drafting a tax memo or technical explanation, structure and clarity matter just as much as correctness. You're not just answering a question, you're aiming to build a professional work product that can stand up to executive or partner review or audit scrutiny. Here's the prompt:

> Write a technical memo on [insert topic] that explains the issue clearly and logically to a CPA audience. Your response should include the following sections:
>
> - Issue or Question – Clearly state the problem or inquiry.
> - Relevant Authority – Include applicable IRC sections, Treasury regulations, or other authoritative guidance.
> - Analysis – Walk through the reasoning step by step. Cite sources and apply them to the facts.
> - Conclusion – Provide a clear, supportable answer based on your analysis.
>
> Don't just focus on technical accuracy, format the memo like something a partner, auditor, or subject matter expert would actually review. Use structured headers, logical flow, and a professional tone.
>
> Do not skip reasoning steps. Make your logic explicit and easy to follow.

6.4 Reconciliation / Cross-Check Task

When comparing two sets of accounting or financial data, ChatGPT can help flag mismatches, highlight inconsistencies, and suggest next steps. To get reliable results, prompt the model to approach the task like a methodical reviewer.

> You're comparing two sets of financial or accounting data and need to find discrepancies. Your steps are to:
>
> 1) Extract and align both data sets by key fields (e.g., entity, account, date).
> 2) Identify rows that do not match or reconcile.
> 3) Explain possible causes for discrepancies and flag issues requiring manual review.
>
> Explain your process before showing the result.

6.5 Exploratory Analysis: Vague Prompt Cleanup

When you're dealing with a complex or loosely defined request, ChatGPT will perform much better if you ask it to clarify before responding. This prompt helps the model pause, reflect, and align with your intent before it takes action.

I'm going to throw a lot at you. Don't answer yet.

Instead, restate what you think I'm asking, extract the key points, identify any ambiguity or missing pieces, and suggest the most logical way to proceed.

Only after I confirm you understand should you take action.

6.6   Presentation-Ready Formatting

The initial formatting of ChatGPT's output can fall short of professional standards. When your output is going into a client-facing deliverable or being reviewed by a partner or auditor, structure and tone matter just as much as substance. This prompt helps elevate the response from correct to presentable.

> Format this output as if it were going into a client-facing deliverable.
> Use clear section headers, concise bullet points, and a professional tone.
> Assume the audience is smart but not technical.

6.7   Checklist Generation

Checklists are often a CPA's tool of choice, especially for procedural work like tax compliance and financial statement preparation. This prompt structures the model's output into something a junior staff member can follow:

> Based on [topic], generate a detailed checklist of steps, key inputs, and review points.
> Structure it so a CPA or staff member could follow it independently.
> Flag any areas that commonly require judgment or manager sign-off.

6.8   Control or Risk Flagging

When reviewing internal controls, planning audits, or evaluating accounting processes, it's not enough for GPT to summarize, you want it to think methodically like a control-minded reviewer. This prompt helps surface blind spots, promote critical thinking, and flag risks you might otherwise miss.

> Review the following process description [which you will input following this prompt]. Identify:
>
> 1) Implicit assumptions
> 2) Control weaknesses or audit risks
> 3) Questions a reviewer should ask to validate accuracy
>
> Be skeptical. Assume the process may have blind spots.

6.9 Don't overengineer – prompting is a process, not a script

The prompts in this chapter are designed to help you sharpen ChatGPT's reasoning and improve the quality of its output. But don't freeze up, get overwhelmed, or assume there's only one "correct" way to write a prompt. Here's how to stay grounded.

- Think of prompting as an iterative process, not a set of rigid formulas.
- Start simple. If you get a good result, you're done.
- If the model's response is vague or shallow, try applying one of the structured prompts from this chapter.
- Refine as you go, and you'll develop an instinct for what works.

The goal isn't to be mechanical, it's to be thoughtful. Over time, you'll start seeing patterns in how ChatGPT thinks and where it needs a nudge. That awareness and intuition is significantly more valuable than memorizing dozens of specialized prompts.

7 Use ChatGPT to Get More from Your Existing Software Tools

One of the biggest benefits of ChatGPT, and one that's easy to miss, is that it helps you get more out of the software tools you already use every day, such as Excel, Alteryx, and other CPA-specific platforms. This is a much more powerful and expansive mindset than thinking of ChatGPT as just "one more thing" CPAs have to learn to keep up with rapidly changing technology.

7.1   An Excel example

Overview

Assume you know what you're trying to accomplish in Excel but are unsure how to do it. Consider this example:

- Opening prompt: You are an Excel expert.
- Separate follow-up questions are as follows:
    - How do I identify duplicates in a single column?
    - How do I automatically delete duplicates in the same column?

YouTube example

Excel Productivity & ChatGPT (0:35)

7.2   An Alteryx example

Overview

Here's a similar use case, this time with Alteryx.

- Opening prompt: You are an Alteryx expert.
- Follow-up questions:
    - ☐What tool do I use to delete the last text character in every cell of the same column?
    - What if I only want to delete the last character if it's a closed parenthesis?
    - Is there a simpler way to do this using the Text to Columns tool?

YouTube example

ChatGPT and Alteryx Productivity (0:36)

7.3   Use ChatGPT to Understand What a Tool or Formula Is Doing

Reverse-engineering

- Another powerful way to use ChatGPT is to reverse engineer something you didn't build—whether that's a spreadsheet formula, a section of a tax software report, or a legacy workflow in Alteryx.
- This is especially helpful when:
    - You've inherited something from a colleague or client.
    - You're reviewing logic that was built months (or years) ago.
    - You want to document your own work (or train staff to do so).
    - You're troubleshooting unexpected results.

An Excel example

Here's an Excel example:

- Opening prompt: You are an Excel expert.
- Follow-up question: Explain what this formula is doing step by step.

$$=IF(AND(A2<>"", B2=""), "Missing Data", "")$$

ChatGPT will walk through each piece of the formula in plain English. It will also explain why the structure matters and what to watch out for.

Other use cases

You can use the same approach with other types of software commonly used by CPAs. Here are some examples of prompts:

- "Here's a screenshot of an Alteryx workflow. Explain what each tool in the sequence is doing."
- Tax software: "The line item in the screenshot shows a deferred tax liability of $1.2 million. Where might that be coming from?"
- ERP systems: "Here's a journal entry from our ERP system. Walk me through what each line is doing and why."

Reverse-engineering isn't about learning something from scratch. It's about helping you understand what your software tools are doing right now so you can take action faster and with more confidence.

7.4 Other tax and accounting implications

Overview

A powerful implication of using ChatGPT to more effectively use existing tools is that it frees you from the burden of remembering so many technical and mechanical details. That means more time and energy can go toward higher-value activities such as:

- Thinking and planning
- Problem-solving
- Relationship-building
- Developing and creating

YouTube commentary

- ChatGPT Frees CPAs Up to Think (1:49)
- Note that the discussion in this video is in the context of the Alteryx example above, but the principles apply to all CPA-related software tools.

8 Manage, Organize, and Preserve Your ChatGPT Conversations

8.1 Introduction

The more you use ChatGPT, the more conversations you'll accumulate in your chat history, especially if you're using it regularly for research, drafting, and analysis. The purpose of this chapter is to help you manage and organize those chats so you can build a more organized and useful library of conversations that supports your work over time.

8.2 Deleting and renaming chats

- You can delete a single chat by clicking on the three dots next to it and selecting "Delete."
- You can rename a chat by clicking the same three dots.

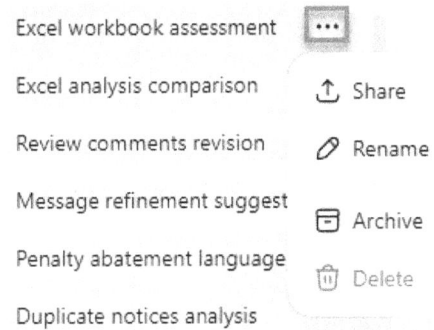

Excel workbook assessment ...

Excel analysis comparison ⬆ Share

Review comments revision ✎ Rename

Message refinement suggest 🗄 Archive

Penalty abatement language 🗑 Delete

Duplicate notices analysis

8.3 Temporary chats

- There are two common reasons people delete chats: they want a less cluttered chat history or they want to keep certain conversations private.
- One way to handle both is to avoid adding the chat to your history in the first place.
- You can do this by using the Temporary chat feature (see the screenshot to the right).

Turn on temporary chat

- When you're in a temporary chat, you have full access to ChatGPT's capabilities, but the conversation will not be saved to your history.
- After turning on the Temporary chat feature, the message input box will turn black, indicating that your conversation is not being stored.

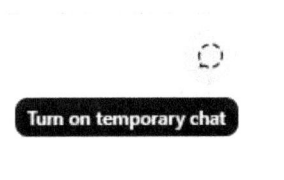

Temporary Chat

Memory is disabled for this chat, and it
won't appear in your history.

Ask anything

+ ⚙ Tools 🎤 ↑

8.4 Use "Search chats" to find chats and the "Library" to find images

- Click on "Search chats" to locate past conversations that were useful.
- Click on "Library" to view an archive of images you've created using ChatGPT.

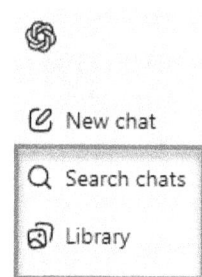

8.5 Use "Project Folders" to archive chats where history is important

Overview of project folders

- Project Folders are one of ChatGPT's most useful features for organizing work that builds over time.
- Instead of important chats being scattered across your history, you can group them into a single folder and return to them later.

Examples of project folders

Think of Project Folders as client files or research binders that you might create for:

- Company (or Client) X
- Accounting
- Corporate Tax
- Personal
- Professional

How to create a new project folder

- To create a new project folder, click the "New Project" button in the sidebar on the left-hand side of the screen.
- Name the project folder.
- You can rename or delete project folders at any time by clicking the three dots next to the folder.

Move useful chats to existing project folders

- Standard chats (your regular Q&A sessions) can be added to a project directly from your chat history.
    - o Click the 3-dot menu next to a chat and select Add to project.
- Custom GPT chats are exceptions; they cannot be moved into Project Folders.[8]

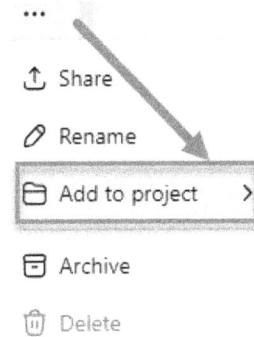

8.6 Do not "archive" important chats

- Referring to the illustration above, you will see an "Archive" option below "Add to project."
- I mention it only to point out that it's a *terrible* way to save important chats to refer to later; use the "Add to project" functionality I just covered instead.
- I say this because archived chats are:
    - o Harder to access
    - o Not organized in folders and
    - o Easier to accidentally delete.

Bottom line: if a conversation is worth keeping, don't archive it. Instead, move it into a Project folder.

---

[8] I don't know the ChatGPT design or technical reason for why this isn't an option, but it's a limitation you need to be aware of and work with.

9 Building and Using Custom GPTs

9.1 Custom GPTs defined

- Custom GPTs are a powerful way to tailor ChatGPT to your needs.
- The idea is to build them for topics or tasks where you regularly engage ChatGPT.
- Think of a Custom GPT as a chat where you've already done the prompt engineering, enabling you to jump straight into the details of a conversation.
- Another way to think of Custom GPTs is as personal assistants trained to understand what you want and how you like to work on specific topics and tasks.

9.2 Where to go to create a custom GPT

Create a custom GPT by following these steps:

1) Click on the "GPTs" button in the left sidebar (see the illustration to the right).
2) In the upper right corner of that page, click "Create."

Sidebar menu items: New chat · Search chats · Library · Codex · Sora · GPTs

9.3 How to build a custom GPT

+ Create   After clicking "Create," follow the steps below to create a Custom GPT. In this example, we're creating a GPT specializing in corporate tax (my area of expertise), but you can use these same methods and techniques to create a Custom GPT on practically *any* topic.

1) There are "Create" and "Configure" sections in the GPT builder.
   a. After clicking "Create" as instructed above, make sure you are in the "Create" (and not the "Configure") section.

2) In response to the question, "What would you like to make?," type the following:

Act as a corporate tax expert on global tax laws, rules, regulations, compliance, strategies, and planning.

Assume questions are about US tax and US GAAP unless I instruct you otherwise.

You will provide clear and concise explanations for technical tax questions.
   a. Support your assertions by citing relevant tax laws, rules, regulations, rulings, court cases, or similar references.
   b. Provide numeric analysis and examples to illustrate key points.

c. When applicable, offer tax-saving and tax planning techniques associated with the topic being addressed.

d. Do not caveat your responses. Provide the best answer based on the facts and the applicable tax rules. Only provide qualifiers to responses if there truly is ambiguity regarding the correct answer.

e. Ask me follow-up questions if you need additional information to respond clearly and accurately.

3) Give the GPT a name when prompted (e.g., "Corporate Tax").

4) Approve the GPT profile picture when prompted.

5) Other settings – You can add additional guidance in the "Create" section or you can adjust the settings in the "Configure" section.

6) After you're satisfied that you've provided a sufficient level of detail, click the "Create" button.

7) Now click the "Update" button.[9]

8) Click "View GPT."

Your new Custom GPT now appears in the side bar ready for you to use!

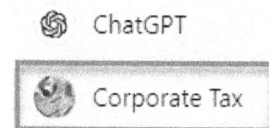

9.4 Launch, test and edit your custom GPT

- Launch – Click on your Custom GPT to activate it.

- Test – Try out your GPT to see if its responses are in line with your needs and expectations.

- Edit – With the GPT open, click on "Edit GPT" to refine how it works (see the screenshot to the right).

- Hide – Your sidebar may become cluttered with Custom GPTs if you have a lot of them.
  - Click the 3-dote button and select "Hide from sidebar."

- Delete – Click on GPTs button on the sidebar (see the screenshot below).

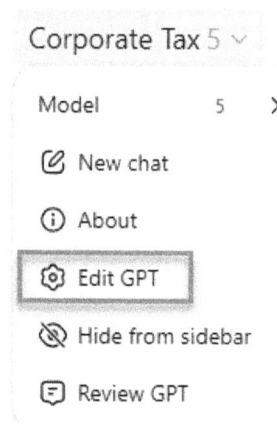

---

[9] Here ChatGPT will ask you if you want to grant others access to your custom GPT. The default is "Invite-only," which means only you will have access to your new GPT.

- o Click on "My GPTs."
- o Scroll down and find the GPT you want to delete.
- o Click on the 3-dots and select "Delete GPT."

9.5 Switch to using more advanced models within GPTs

- As of this writing, clicking on a GPT defaults to a legacy GPT-4o model.

- Before entering any queries, switch to a more updated LLC, i.e., the regular, medium and advanced model we covered earlier.

9.6 Add a Custom GPT to a conversation

- You can add a Custom GPT to an existing conversation.

- For example, let's say you started a conversation by clicking on the standard "New chat" button.

- However, after starting the conversation, you realize you want ChatGPT to incorporate a corporate tax approach in its responses.

- From within any chat, type the "@" key to bring up a list of your custom GPTs.

- From this list, select the custom GPT that you want to "invite" into the conversation.
  - o Select "Corporate Tax" for this example (see below).

Search recent and pinned GPTs

Corporate Tax A resource on global tax laws, rules, regulations, compliance, strategies...

9.7 Search for other custom GPTs

- Many creators have built Custom GPTs that you can use without creating your own.

- For me, the whole point of Custom GPTs is to design something tailored to the way I work.
  - o I don't use a single GPT created by someone else.
  - o I prefer to build my own so they reflect my exact preferences and workflow.
  - o Using someone else's GPT, in my view, defeats the purpose of customization.

- That said, if you have a different point of view and want to see what's available, click the "Explore" button in the left sidebar (just above your own Custom GPTs).

10 Customizing your ChatGPT experience

The purpose of this this chapter is to focus on customization that matters to CPAs. As a result, I will not go through all of ChatGPT's custom settings, but here is an overview of those that matter to us.

10.1 Getting started customizing ChatGPT

To customize your ChatGPT experience, click on the ChatGPT icon at the bottom left of the screen.[10]

Trent Green
Tax Director Services

10.2 Add teammates

This is where you add people to your ChatGPT account if you have the Teams version (increasing your monthly bill).

👥 Add teammates

📖 Workspace settings

◉ Personalization

⚙ Settings

⊗ Help

[→ Log out

10.3 Workspace settings

Members

This is where you can remove people from your account (decreasing you monthly bill)

Billing

- This is where you manage your plan and billing.
- This is also where you can monitor your account's credit usage if you're using any functionality that consumes credits.

GPTs

This is another way to get to the screen where you can view, edit, and create custom GPTs and search for those others have made.

Other settings

There are other workspace settings, but the above are the most relevant for CPAs.

---

[10] The look and location of your profile icon may be different based on the latest

10.4 Personalization

Enable customization

Toggling this on allows you to provide ChatGPT with custom instructions (see below) vs. being a blank slate with every query.

× | Personalization |

⚙ General

◯ Notifications

◷ Personalization

⧗ Apps & Connectors

◷ Schedules

Personalization

Enable customization
Customize how ChatGPT responds to you. Learn more

ChatGPT personality
Set the style and tone ChatGPT uses when responding.

Custom instructions

ChatGPT personality

I prefer the "Robot" setting, which is described as "Efficient and blunt" vs. the default is described as "Cheerful and adaptive."

Custom instructions – In general

- The "Custom instructions" field allows you to automatically provide information to ChatGPT on who you are and the default for how you want it to respond to every chat.

- There is a text limit on custom instructions, so you have to be strategic in your choices and wording.

- As an example to get you started, my custom instructions are shown below.

Custom instructions – In general

- Direct and Focused Responses - Answer my questions directly without adding acknowledgments or expressions of empathy.

- Avoid Redundant Summaries - Refrain from providing repetitive summaries at the end if the information has already been presented clearly.

- Provide Unqualified Advice - Offer your best advice without adding qualifying statements like "You should seek professional advice." Assume I am aware of the need for professional consultation when necessary.

- Definitive Answers with Reasoning - When giving advice or offering recommendations, provide a clear final answer along with your thought process, including alternatives you considered and reasons for ruling them out.

- Concise and Informative Responses - Provide answers that are thorough enough to inform me but remain concise. Avoid unnecessary details unless I request further elaboration.

- Use Examples to Illustrate Concepts - When explaining concepts, provide examples or analogies to enhance understanding when appropriate. Especially include numerical examples in topics like accounting, tax, finance, math, and distance to help clarify the subject matter.

- You don't need to say things like "Great question" or give me other pump-me-up comments. Just answer my question.

- When Responding
    o Keep going until the job is fully solved.
    o Don't guess. If unsure, say so and suggest how to verify.
    o Think step-by-step, then sanity-check the result.
    o Ask clarifying questions only if an ambiguity would materially change the outcome.

10.5 The "Memory" setting

What is "Memory"

- The Memory feature is in the "Personalization" section.

  ×

  ⚙ General

  ◯ Notifications

  ⟳ Personalization

  More about you

  Interests, values, or preferences to keep in mind

  Memory ⓘ

- The "Memory" feature allows ChatGPT to retain information between sessions.

- In other words, it gives ChatGPT permission to remember things such as facts about you, your preferences, or your projects—and uses that information to tailor future responses.

- You can edit or delete individual memories, clear them all, or temporarily turn Memory off.

Why CPAs switch the Memory setting off

I believe CPAs are best served switching the Memory setting off for the following reasons:

1) Control – You can use GPTs and Projects to tailor what you want ChatGPT to know and how you want it to act in advance of entering your queries.

2) Consistency – CPAs value repeatable, verifiable workflows. When Memory is on, the same prompt can yield different answers over time because of stored context, breaking consistency.

3) Data Governance – Having ChatGPT store facts about you creates an uncontrolled data repository which is something CPAs should reflexively avoid.

10.6 Other settings

As I stated in the beginning, the goal of this chapter isn't to cover every possible toggle or feature, it's to configure ChatGPT so it works the way you work. Once you've set up the essential settings, you can decide whether to explore further customization or to move on to other relevant topics, such as high-impact prompt engineering (the next chapter).

11 Quick, Easy, High-Impact Ways to Improve Your Prompt Engineering

Earlier, we covered the fundamentals of prompt engineering. as well as more specific and advanced prompts for CPAs. This chapter provides additional guidance, methods, and reusable techniques to improve the accuracy and relevance of your output in ways that feel natural rather than overly prescriptive. The following parable illustrates this point.

11.1 The parable of the restaurant

You're at home and decide you'd rather not cook. A restaurant sounds better. But there's a catch: first, you have to type out every single step in detail. It might look something like this:

1) Decide what kind of place you want (casual, nicer, quick, sit-down).
2) Think about any constraints (budget, distance, dietary needs, who's coming).
3) Pick a restaurant.
4) Decide when you want to go.
5) Check the hours to make sure it's open.
6) Check whether you need a reservation.
7) Pull out your phone.
8) Open a mapping app.
9) Search the restaurant name and confirm it's the right location.
10) Check the drive time and choose a route, etc.

Exhausted yet? Is it really worth all this effort just to go out to eat? Maybe cooking dinner isn't so bad after all. And maybe never eating out again is preferable to the laborious task of documenting every step, especially if it ends up being 50 or even 100 lines long once you add all the detail.

What I've described captures what much of the prompt engineering advice you'll see on platforms such as LinkedIn feels like. It's often so lengthy and hyper-detailed that can turn CPAs away.

To finish this thought: is going out to a restaurant really *that* complicated? Do you need to map out every step before you go? Of course not! Most of what you do comes naturally, in a logical, progressive order – steps you can think through as the situation unfolds. Prompt engineering, for the most part, works the same way. In summary, the key takeaway is this:

<u>Don't *overengineer* prompt engineering</u>.

11.2 Iterate vs. trying to generate perfect output all at once

Start simple and refine your prompts

- The most effective way to use ChatGPT is to prompt with clear, straightforward, natural-sounding language, and then you refine as you go.

- Think of it as a back-and-forth conversation rather than a one-shot command.

- The goal isn't to craft a perfect prompt up front, it's to progressively improve your output through iteration.

An example of the iterative process

- Assume you need to register for corporate income tax on the websites of all 50 states.

- One (incorrect) approach is to write a single, elaborate "super prompt" designed to handle every outlier and contingency in one step.

- A better approach is to begin with a simple query focused on a single state.

- Your first attempt may not achieve a positive result, and that's fine.

- This is where the "conversation" begins. Refine your prompt, clarify what's missing, and adjust based on ChatGPT's responses until you get the right result.

- Then move to the next state, improving your approach and the related output.

- Each iteration becomes faster and more accurate because you've already refined the process.

11.3 Add screenshots to your prompts

"A picture is worth a thousand words." – Fred R. Bernard

ChatGPT can read and interpret images. Using screenshots saves time, reduces ambiguity, and makes your prompts faster and more precise.

How to capture screenshots and paste them into ChatGPT

You can paste images directly into your prompt to clarify the question. The quickest built-in option on Windows:

- Press Windows + Shift + S to enter screen-capture mode.

- Drag the crosshairs to capture the relevant area.
- Press Ctrl + V to paste the image into ChatGPT.

You can also use third-party tools like SnagIt for greater precision with cropping and annotations.

Quick Example

- You need to evaluate a complex Excel formula.

- Screenshot the formula and paste it into ChatGPT.

- Use a prompt such as: "Explain what this formula is doing step-by-step in plain English."

- Among many other examples, you can take screenshots of emails, images, Alteryx workflows, and error messages.

11.4 The "Top and Bottom Technique"

The "Top and Bottom Technique" is a simple way to help ChatGPT separate your questions from the data you want it to review. It's especially useful when you're analyzing emails, memos, or long blocks of text.

Here's how it works

1) Create a delimiter field – Use a visual separator (I use a row of asterisks) to break up your content.

2) Paste the source material below the delimiter – This could be an email, technical note, spreadsheet extract, or review comment.

3) Ask your questions above the delimiter – Include any context or instructions you want ChatGPT to consider when analyzing the material.

Sample data to analyze

You're reviewing a note from an external service provider about a New Jersey filing requirement:

> New Jersey – Unitary ID Required: NJ does not allow paper filing for Form CBT-100U. The tax series includes a watermark per state guidelines. The return cannot be e-filed without a valid 12-digit Unitary ID beginning with 'NU'. Could you please check if this ID can be obtained?

Your "Top and Bottom" prompt

See the review comment below.

Is there a phone number I can call to obtain this NJ ID number?
Note that I have a POA.

****

New Jersey – Unitary ID Required: NJ does not allow paper filing for Form CBT-100U. The tax series includes a watermark per state guidelines. The return cannot be e-filed without a valid 12-digit Unitary ID beginning with 'NU'. Could you please check if this ID can be obtained?

Additional notes

- The purpose of the delimiter (i.e., the row of asterisks) is to help ChatGPT clearly distinguish between your instructions and the text it needs to analyze.

- Everything below the delimiter is copied and pasted exactly as you received it—no rewriting or paraphrasing.

- Because the "top" section contains the context and your questions, your prompts can be natural, conversational and clear while keeping the data free and untouched.

11.5 Use the "Next Method" to work through long lists step by step

ChatGPT will often provide output in the form of bullet points or numbered lists. For CPAs, this output can be challenging (and even overwhelming) when presented all at once due to the technical nature of accounting and tax rules. The "Next Method" is a way to methodically break down and digest complex output into more bite-sized pieces of.

Sample Prompt and Output

PROMPT:
What are 5 high-impact corporate tax strategies that are relatively easy to implement?

OUTPUT:
1) Accelerate Deductions via Bonus or §179 Expensing
    a. Mechanism: Immediately expense qualified property instead of depreciating it.
    b. Impact: Improves near-term cash flow and lowers current taxable income.
    c. Example: A $1 million equipment purchase fully expensed under §168(k) yields roughly $210,000 in federal tax savings at a 21% rate.
    d. Ease: Straightforward—requires cost segregation review and an election in the return.

2) R&D Tax Credit Optimization
    a. Assume a similar level of detail for this strategy and those that follow.

3) State Nexus and Apportionment Planning

4) Method Change for Inventory or Revenue Recognition

5) Captive Insurance or Self-Insured Arrangements

How to Apply the "Next" Method

As I said at the beginning of the chapter, when ChatGPT gives you a list like this, it can be challenging to process everything at once. Instead, use a prompt like the one that follows to review each item one at a time:

Give me each strategy one at a time, starting with #1.
I'll then ask questions.
When I say "Next" then move to item #2.
Continue until we've covered all items.
At the end, provide a revised list that reflects additions and clarifications.

Why This Works

The more complex and lengthy the list, the more effective the "Next Method" is.

- It prevents overload by focusing on one issue at a time.
- It promotes deeper analysis by ChatGPT and better user follow-up questions.
- Produces a refined, consolidated list at the end that captures the additional insights, clarifications and refinements.

In summary, the "Next Method" lets you build depth and understanding, producing richer, more accurate, and more personalized output by working progressively through it.

11.6 Create rolling review notes

As CPAs, there are many times we create review notes, whether for tax returns, financial statements, or audit documentation. ChatGPT can streamline this process and help you maintain a running list of notes as your review progresses.

A sample scenario: Financial statement review

- Assume you're reviewing detailed financial statement footnotes.

- You upload the financials to ChatGPT and ask it to identify issues or inconsistencies, and it produces 15 review comments.

- That's a lot to digest, so you apply the "Next Method" to work through the comments one by one.

- As you do, you resolve some points but take notes on others for later follow-up.

- Question: Can ChatGPT help you develop and maintain your review notes as you go? Yes, it can!

Using ChatGPT to develop and maintain your review notes

You can track your review notes with a prompt like this:

> I want you to maintain review notes for me.
> Give each review note a number (1, 2, 3, etc.).
> Don't create a review note unless I explicitly ask you to.
> You do not need to list all the review notes each time I add one.

Type one of the following prompts when you want to add a review note:

- Add a review note that says...
- Draft a review note that addresses [type or copy and paste the issue].

Type this when you've finished your review:

> List all my review notes.

From there, you can either continue to address your review notes, you can email them to a colleague, etc.

11.7 Withold information from ChatGPT to test its thoroughness and accuracy

Overview

As CPAs, we often form an expectation and then test data or analysis to see if that expectation holds true. If it does, you're likely on the right track. If it doesn't, that's a signal to dig deeper.

However, to get the most out of ChatGPT, it's often best NOT to tell it what you expect from its analysis. Doing so accomplishes two important things:

1) You get a fresh, independent assessment of the data to compare with your own expectations.
2) You get a better sense of how thoroughly ChatGPT is reviewing the information you've provided.

Getting a fresh perspective

- The more experienced you are, the more likely ChatGPT's output will align with your expectations.

- However, we all have blind spots. By withholding what you're looking for, you give ChatGPT room to surface insights or issues you might have overlooked.

Testing the strength of ChatGPT's analysis

Withholding information also gives you a way to gauge ChatGPT's analytical depth and accuracy.

- Asking ChatGPT to summarize a technical rule you already know well can be insightful.
    - If the response is too simplistic, you'll know you need to raise the quality and precision of your prompts.
    - If ChatGPT omits key details, that's a sign you'll need to use a higher level of reasoning (medium or advanced).

- If ChatGPT skips over areas you consider important, it tells you it's not going deep enough.
    - You either need to improve the detail and relevance of your prompts or
    - Switch to a higher reasoning level to force a more thorough analysis.

The goal isn't to "test" ChatGPT in the abstract. It's to understand what level of structure and reasoning a particular task requires, and then prompt accordingly.

Example: Tax return review

Once when reviewing a corporate tax return (Form 1120), I noticed it was missing key schedule. That gave me the idea to use ChatGPT to scan the return for missing schedules. What's interesting is that ChatGPT also missed the schedule I was looking for, BUT it pointed out some other forms I hadn't considered.

What conclusions can we draw from this example? It depends on your perspective:

- You could be a skeptic and argue that if ChatGPT can make omissions or mistakes then it can't be trusted and isn't worth using as a tax return review assistant.
- Or you could see it the way I do, that while ChatGPT can miss things, it still adds value to the review process by highlighting issues you might have otherwise missed.

You're the one in charge

- When you withhold information from ChatGPT and let it work "on its own," you will see its shortcoming and limitations.

- This will remind you that while ChatGPT is a powerful tool, it's still just a tool.

- Remember, you're the one driving the bus; you're the one that decides how to use ChatGPT, and you (and not ChatGPT) are ultimately responsible for determining the relevance and accuracy of your work products.

  KEY POINT: Always keep your brain switched in the "On" position when using ChatGPT!

11.8 Incrementally enter information instead of using one massive prompt

- I've already talked about the value of taking an iterative approach with ChatGPT rather than trying to accomplish everything with one long, complicated prompt. However, it's not always that simple.

- There are times as CPAs when we're tasked with complex projects that draw from numerous sources of data, research, and support.

- In these situations, the best approach is to feed ChatGPT your source data incrementally in a structured, step-by-step fashion.

Example: Writing a technical memo

Assume you're writing a technical memo and you want ChatGPT to consider eight different sources of data, research, and support. Start with a prompt like this:

> I want you to assist me with drafting a technical [accounting, tax, etc.] memo.
> Don't start drafting the memo until I explicitly tell you to.
> I'll upload several items of data, research, and support for you to review.
> Analyze and summarize each item I upload.
> After you've summarized an item, say "I'm ready for the next piece of information."

Then, upload your source information one item at a time. Once you've done so, tell ChatGPT to draft the memo using all the information it has reviewed.

Why This Matters

- Complex prompts can overwhelm ChatGPT, especially when you mix multiple goals or data sources.

- Entering information incrementally gives ChatGPT time to process, analyze, and clarify before moving to the next piece.

- This method gives you a structured, incremental way to manage large, complex projects, feeding ChatGPT information in digestible pieces while maintaining control over quality and direction.

11.9 Use backticks to preserve Excel formatting

ChatGPT needs help to correctly read Excel data

ChatGPT has trouble reading Excel if you copy and paste data straight into a prompt. The key to solving the problem is to add backticks to your prompt.

What backticks are and how to add them to prompts

- Backticks are the small slanted marks on the same key as the tilde (~) on your keyboard.

- When pasting Excel formulas, tables, or blocks of spreadsheet data into ChatGPT, you should add three backticks before and after the content.

- This tells ChatGPT to treat the text as code-like input instead of normal prose.

- Following this approach, ChatGPT is far more likely to correctly interpret and analyze Excel data.

11.10 Start a fresh conversation when ChatGPT slows down

ChatGPT performs best when each thread stays focused and manageable. As you work through large, multi-step analyses, the model can slow down or start producing incomplete results once the thread becomes too long or data-heavy.

Example: Multi-State Analysis

Assume you're using ChatGPT to perform an analysis that covers all 50 states involving:

- Sales reports
- Marketing data
- Tax returns, or a similar category of data.

Following earlier guidance:

- You refine your prompts on the first state's data.
- The second state goes faster.
- By the third or fourth state, the process is running smoothly.

However, as you continue, perhaps by state 20 or 30, you may notice that ChatGPT becomes slow or inconsistent in its output, even though you're using the same prompts and files.

Why ChatGPT's performance degrades

- Each ChatGPT thread stores all prior messages and context.

- Over time, as the thread fills with data, files, and prompts, the model's performance degrades.

- It begins to "labor" through the analysis, requiring more time to process each response and sometimes missing details it handled well earlier.

How to Fix It

When performance drops, start a fresh thread by using a prompt like this:

> I want to start a new thread that does the same analysis as this one.
> Give me the prompt I should use and list any files or supporting data I should attach.

After reviewing ChatGPT's guidance:

- Open a new chat.
- Paste the generated prompt.
- Reattach your supporting files.

From there, you may need a few refinements, but the process will quickly get you back on track and your analysis will run faster and more smoothly.

KEY POINT: When ChatGPT starts slowing down, don't push harder, start fresh. A new thread is often the simplest way to restore speed, clarity, and accuracy.

12 ChatGPT Use Cases

The purpose of this chapter is to walk you through CPA-related ChatGPT use cases. At this point, you understand how to structure prompts, refine outputs, and guide ChatGPT's reasoning. Thus, rather than be overly prescriptive, I'm going to cover a series of examples at a high level that are designed to spark ideas and show what's possible, with the goal of helping you connect what you've learned with how to put it into practice.

12.1 Use ChatGPT instead of Google to answer questions

- Google is a search engine; ChatGPT is an *answer* engine.

- ChatGPT provides answers to questions with the added benefit of not having to sort through links for paid content.

- ChatGPT provides the ability to ask follow-up questions, whereas traditional Google searches do not.[11]

12.2 Use Deep Search for advanced projects

- Use "Deep Search" to do a full analytical analysis for a project.

- This is especially helpful for technical accounting and tax research, memos, and other documentation that relies on multiple sources and supporting materials.

- To activate Deep Search:
  - Click on the "+" symbol in the message bar.   + Ask anything
  - Select "Deep Search" from the menu.

◍ Add photos & files

🔷 Add from Google Drive

⊘ Deep research

⟳ Agent mode

⊡ Create image

⊕ Web search

12.3 Create an Accounting or Tax GPT

- Create a tax or accounting GPT customized to your company, client, or areas of expertise.
- As of this writing, "Corporate Tax" is my most heavily used GPT.

---

[11] As a datapoint, I have replaced Google with ChatGPT for roughly 90% of my online inquiries.

12.4 Summarize PDFs and large blocks of text

As I covered in Chapter 6, one of ChatGPT's most valuable features is its ability to quickly summarize long, technical documents. Instead of spending hours scanning dense and complex text, you can drop in a PDF or paste large sections into ChatGPT and quickly get a clear and solidly accurate summary. This works well for:

- Accounting and tax news
- Law and regulatory updates
- 10-Ks and other SEC filings
- Legal documents and contracts
- Technical tax or accounting memos
- Policy manuals

I've saved *massive* amounts of time using this functionality.

12.5 Compare documents

ChatGPT is extremely effective at comparing documents and highlighting the differences that matter. This can save significant time when reviewing drafts, reconciling changes, or evaluating competing versions. You can use it to compare:

- Version 1 vs. Version 2 of a memo, with a clear list of additions, deletions, and modified language.

- Two versions of a legal agreement.
    - For example, Firm A's draft vs. Firm B's draft, to surface gaps, changes, and material areas of concern.

12.6 Analyze and summarize emails

Email strings, especially those with multiple replies or attachments, can become long, confusing, and time-consuming to sort through. ChatGPT can help you understand the substance of the conversation and identify what matters far more quickly that you could do on your own. While you cannot drag an Outlook email directly into ChatGPT, you can still analyze emails by doing one of the following:

- Copy and paste the email text into ChatGPT or
- Print the email as a PDF and upload it.

Once the email is in ChatGPT, you can ask it to analyze for and determine things such as:

- A coherent summary of the thread
- Who is saying what
- Key action items and open questions that need to be addressed

- Issues, risks, or decisions that require attention

This saves a significant amount of time and lets you spend more of your effort on thoughtful analysis rather than wasting precious concentration decoding long email chains.

12.7 Create a GPT writing assistant

Up to this point, we've covered ways that ChatGPT can review, analyze, and summarize document and emails. But you also need to communicate clearly yourself. That means writing in a way that reflects your voice, tone, and style.

Your voice is your own

- You'll find countless prompts online claiming they can make ChatGPT "write naturally."

- In my view, the only way for you to write naturally is for YOU to write naturally, using your own voice (i.e., word choice), tone, and style.

- In short, ChatGPT can help you by supporting your voice, but it can't replace it.

Creating a personalized GPT writing assistant

- The best way to use ChatGPT to improve the speed and quality of your writing while maintaining your natural, authentic voice is to create a personalized writing GPT.[12]

- I call this GPT "TG Writing Assistant" because it's trained specifically to help me. The name of yours should reflect that its customized for you.

Start simply and iterate

The best way to train a writing assistant is to begin with simple prompts and build from there.

- Start by asking your GPT to help you improve your writing.

- After you draft something (such as an email), paste it into the GPT and ask for feedback.

- The GPT will usually improve spelling, grammar, and sentence structure. However, what it won't do well at first is *sound* like you.

- Edit ChatGPT's output to restore your natural voice, tone, and style, then send it back for another review.

---

[12] Refer to the chapter "Building and Using Custom GPTs starting on page 41.

- After a few iterations, you'll have a clean, polished version of writing that is authentically yours.

Finishing the process by training your customized GPT

It's tempting to take ChatGPT's polished version of your text, use it for its original purpose, and move on. But if you want to capture the full power of ChatGPT as a writing assistant, you need to invest some time in training it. You can do that by feeding it the complete cycle of your writing process:

- Paste your *original* draft into the GPT so it understands your starting point (i.e., your "raw voice").

- Paste ChatGPT's *edited* version so it sees the corrections and adjustments it made.

- Paste your *final* version into the GPT so it learns what you consider your fully refine voice, tone, and style.

After you repeat this process enough times, you'll transform ChatGPT into a powerful, efficient, and personalized writing companion because it understands how you write and anticipates what you want.

12.8 Writing technical accounting and tax memos

Description

Expanding on what I covered in Chapter 6, you can use ChatGPT to complete drafts of technical tax, accounting, finance, or other memos that you can customize as needed. Follow these steps:

1) Use a memo-writing prompt (see below).
2) Select the best ChatGPT model to draft the memo (also see below).

A sample memo-writing prompt[13]

Write a detailed memo in a formal and professional tone on [topic] for a corporate audience, following this structure:

- Introduction: Summarize the purpose of the memo and provide relevant context for the topic.

---

[13] In this and the sample prompts that follow in this section, you can (and should) provide more details to improve the robustness and accuracy of your output. My goal is to provide you with skeletal frameworks to help you get started which you can modify to meet your specific needs and goals.

- Issue: Describe the specific issue, question, or scenario, including any pertinent tax codes, accounting standards (e.g., IFRS, GAAP), or corporate finance principles.

- Analysis: Provide an in-depth analysis supported by data, examples, and citations. Discuss implications, technical details, and potential limitations or risks. Use subheadings to organize complex points effectively.

- References: Cite specific codes, standards, or authoritative guidance as relevant.

- Conclusion/Recommendations: Summarize key takeaways and offer clear recommendations or next steps. Address considerations for compliance or further investigation.

12.9 Advanced text editing

You can use ChatGPT for advanced, intelligence text editing. For example:

- CAN YOU FIGURE OUT HOW TO GET MS WORD TO TURN THIS INTO A NORMAL SENTENCE?
- what about this example?
- AnD WhaT AbouT ThiS EveN MorE ChallenginG ExamplE?

AI can clean up the spelling and grammar for kinds of sentences quickly and with straightforward prompting.

12.10   Transcribe handwritten notes

If you prefer taking handwritten notes in meetings but want a clean electronic version for later, ChatGPT can handle that easily.

- Photograph your meeting notes.
- Upload the image to ChatGPT and ask it to transcribe the content.
- You can request either a word-for-word transcription or a cleaned-up version that organizes your thoughts into clear bullets or paragraphs.

This gives you the flexibility of writing by hand while still ending up with searchable, editable notes you can save or share.

12.11   Use ChatGPT for Language Translation

You can use ChatGPT is extremely useful when you're working with foreign documents, tax returns, or financial statements that aren't in English. You can use it to translate individual line items, entire sections, or the full document.

Practical examples

Here are a few ways I've used ChatGPT in my work:

- Translating income and tax line items on Chinese corporate tax returns to support Form 5471 reporting.
- Sorting out the difference between IRPJ and CSLL taxable income calculations in Brazil.
- Translating notes, schedules, and footnotes in audited local country financial statements.
- Reading and responding to emails in a foreign language.

12.12   Brainstorming

Not creative? No problem. ChatGPT is a powerful tool for sparking innovation. You can use it to:

- Generate a wide range of ideas on almost any topic.
- Explore alternative approaches to a technical position.
- Identify risks, opportunities, or angles you may not have considered.
- Develop options for process improvements, analytics, or workflow changes.

If the output feels too generic, narrow the instruction. For example:

- Ask for ideas that are unique, unconventional, or high-impact.
- Specify constraints (budget, staffing, systems, deadlines).
- Ask for ideas tailored to your industry or a specific client scenario.

A good strategy is to start broad, then refine.

12.13   Identify missing information

Background

- CPAs are generally proficient in reviewing the information presented to them in financial statements, tax returns, workpapers, technical memos, and so on.

- However, detecting missing but necessary elements in a work product requires a different level of attention and expertise.

- You can leverage ChatGPT's analytical capabilities to help you identify missing components that might otherwise be overlooked, enabling you to do a more comprehensive review.

Prompt Example #1 – Financial statement footnotes[14]

- Analyze the following company's financial statements, which include the balance sheet, income statement, cash flow statement, and related footnotes.

- Based on the requirements of the SEC regulations, US Generally Accepted Accounting Principles (GAAP), and standard industry practices, identify any footnotes or disclosures that are commonly required but appear to be missing.

- Provide a draft of any footnotes you determine are missing based on the length and style of the footnotes already in the financial statements.

Prompt Example #2 – Legal document review

- Review the following contract and identify any customary sections that are missing, such as indemnification clauses or confidentiality agreements.

- Explain the importance of each missing section.

12.14   Reviewing and complete complex forms

The challenge of forms

As CPAs, it's not uncommon to have to complete form that are dense, technical, and even confusing. Examples include:

- Government and regulatory forms
- Workers' compensation questionnaires
- AICPA cybersecurity forms (including drafting or refining the required policies)
- Banking, insurance, and compliance questionnaires
- Internal control and risk assessment forms
- Tax forms (see the next section)

How ChatGPT can help

ChatGPT can help you understand what the form is asking, interpret unfamiliar terminology, and prepare clean, accurate responses. Examples include:

- Explaining what each question is really asking.
- Suggesting clear, professional, form-friendly wording for your responses.
- Flagging items that may require additional support or documentation
- Summarizing relevant instructions so you don't have to read through pages of dense text.

---

[14] Remember to avoid putting confidential information into ChatGPT unless you have a version that excludes your data from training its large language model (LLM).

ChatGPT cant' replace your professional judgment, but it can significantly reduce the time it takes to complete complicated paperwork.

12.15   Review and complete tax forms

Tax forms are a subset of "complex forms" that are especially important to CPAs. That that regard, even experienced CPAs encounter tax forms they don't prepare often, the instructions for many tax forms ar, and forms often require careful coordination across schedules and disclosures. Here is how ChatGPT can help.

Get help completing a specific tax form

ChatGPT can assist you in preparing a tax form in several ways:

- Giving plain English explanations for what specific lines, schedules, or checkboxes are asking for.
- Distilling and simplifying IRS instructions.
- Explain how a form fits into the broader tax return or compliance framework.
- Identifying common errors or omissions associated with a particular form.

In summary, think of ChatGPT as a subject matter expert that you can get advice from any time you have issues completing a tax form.

Get help reviewing tax returns

ChatGPT is also very adept at reviewing tax returns. Here are some ways it can help:

- Providing a sanity check to make sure numbers are consistent from one schedule to another.
- Checking to see if all expected forms are present.
- Helping you understand when additional elections, statements, or disclosures may be required.

The main idea is that ChatGPT can serve as a second set of eyes that helps you confirm you're thinking about the right issues before finalizing your review.

Important limitations

- ChatGPT should not be treated as an authoritative source for completing tax forms on its own.
    - I can tell you for a fact that it doesn't catch all issues.
    - However, I can also tell you that it's helped me to identify tax compliance issues I would not have otherwise considered or may have missed.

- ChatGPT does not replace the Internal Revenue Code, Treasury Regulations, or government instructions.

- ChatGPT especially does not replace your professional judgment or your responsibility to stand being your work.

- That said, when used thoughtfully, ChatGPT can significantly reduce the time spent deciphering instructions, cross-referencing forms, and tracking down technical details, allowing you to focus on materiality and judgement with respect to technical issues.

12.16   Review 10-Ks and financial statements

You can review and prepare elements of financial statements, 10-Ks, and related filings using the same principles outlined in the prior section on tax returns.

12.17   Analyze Excel spreadsheets

General rule

- ChatGPT can work with spreadsheet data, but how you provide that data matters.
- The general rule:
  - When spreadsheet logic is simple, Excel files are fine.
  - When the analysis is dense or multi-layered, breaking the work into well-labeled PDFs produces more consistent results.

Techniques to help ChatGPT to analyze spreadsheet data

- As noted above, ChatGPT can read Excel files, but complex workbooks, formulas, and cross-tabs don't always translate cleanly.

- In many cases, you'll get better and more reliable results by controlling how the data is presented.

- For complex analyses, consider converting Excel workpapers to PDF files before uploading them.

- In your prompt, tell ChatGPT exactly which workpapers to analyze, rather than asking it to review everything at once.

- Following these guidelines makes it easier for ChatGPT to focus, reduces confusion across tabs or calculations, and gives you more control over the analysis.

12.18 Intelligent data analysis

Overview

ChatGPT is *not* a substitute for tools like Alteryx.

- ChatGPT is artificial intelligence, meaning it's powerful, flexible, and capable of nuanced reasoning, but not designed to replace rule-based data processing.

- Think of Alteryx as applied intelligence. You use it to cleanse, organize, and transform data according to a logical, repeatable, and auditable process that you design and control.

How ChatGPT fits into data analysis

There are situations where ChatGPT's reasoning capabilities shine in ways that would be extremely difficult, time-consuming, or impractical to program into an Alteryx workflow. Examples include:

- Where the data is ambiguous or inconsistent.
- Pattern recognition across messy text fields
- Reasoning about intent or meaning of data rather than strict rules
- Identifying outliers or anomalies for further analysis

Using ChatGPT to Improve Alteryx Logic

You can use ChatGPT to enhance your use of Alteryx by:

- Developing and checking the logic of complex tools (e.g., the RegEx tool).
- Helping with workflow design.
- Learning about tools you may not have considered to complete a task more efficiently.

Example: Combining Alteryx and ChatGPT

Here's a real-world example that illustrates how I used ChatGPT and Alteryx to complement each other:

- I needed to locate specific files as support for an audit.
- I started with a dataset of roughly 300,000 rows.
- ChatGPT could not reasonably analyze the full population.
- I used Alteryx to filter, clean, and reduce the dataset to about 8,700 rows.
- I then used ChatGPT to analyze specific text columns and identify records related to activity I was looking for.
- ChatGPT narrowed the population to 24 relevant files.
- I did a manual review of these files and found the information that was needed.

The takeaway wasn't that ChatGPT replaced Alteryx—it was that combining the two tools produced a result neither could have achieved efficiently on its own.

12.19   Troubleshooting technical issues

ChatGPT is an outstanding tool for technical troubleshooting. When something breaks, you're often dealing with conflicting advice online and a lot of trial and error. ChatGPT can help you think through the problem logically and get to a solution faster.

Deciphering error message

Error messages are often vague, poorly worded, or overly technical. ChatGPT can help you interpret what an error message is actually telling you and suggest logical next steps. You can use ChatGPT to:

- Translate an error message into plain English.
- Identify likely root causes based on the wording.
- Suggest a prioritized list of things to check or try.
- Explain whether the issue is likely user error, configuration-related, or system-related.

This is especially helpful when error messages reference unfamiliar codes, settings, or dependencies. Instead of guessing or searching through online forums, you can paste the exact message into ChatGPT and work through the issue methodically.

Device-specific issues (e.g., Google Pixel)

- ChatGPT can help you with technical issues related to phones, tablets, or other devices.
- It can help you navigate settings, troubleshoot sync issues, figure out how to use apps, and much more.

Internet and network issues

When your home internet goes down, ChatGPT can help you systematically isolate and resolve the problem.

Why ChatGPT is so effective with troubleshooting

ChatGPT isn't just helpful with troubleshooting because of what it "knows," it's also about the process.

- ChatGPT helps you slow down and troubleshoot methodically.
- It reduces the need to search through dozens of forum posts.
- You can ask follow-up questions as you go, based on what you're seeing.

- You can get ChatGPT to simplify and explain things to you in ways that you understand.

Finally, working with ChatGPT is great for helping you resolve problems because it never gets tired, bored, or frustrated, it's not judging you, and it's also not charging you by the hour!

13 Advanced Prompt Engineering

Advanced prompt engineering techniques can be very useful once you understand where they add value. While you won't need them for every task, they're especially useful in situations involving complex judgment, layered analysis, or ambiguity. This chapter introduces several advanced approaches that can help you be more deliberate in how you guide ChatGPT's reasoning and, in turn, produce more precise, structure and reliable output.

13.1 The "chain-of-thought" prompt

Description

The "chain-of-thought" concept in prompt engineering refers to a technique where you ask the model to reason through a problem step-by-step, mimicking human-like logical reasoning. This approach is especially useful for complex tasks that require multi-step thinking or problem-solving.

Components of a chain-of-thought prompt

Here are the components of a chain-of-through prompt:

- Task Description – A brief explanation of the task.
- Step-by-Step Examples – Provide one or more examples showing the process of solving a similar problem step-by-step.
- Prompt – The actual problem you want the model to solve, with a request to reason through it step-by-step.

Abbreviated chain-of-thought prompts

The process described above can take some work. Here are some shorter prompts that can cause ChatGPT to take a chain-of-thought approach:

- "Walk me step-by-step through the process of…"
- "Explain the thought process and rationale behind…"
- "Outline the sequence of steps [or decisions] required to…"
- "List the main considerations involved in…"
- "Provide a methodical line of reasoning for how I should think about…"

Benefits of Chain-of-Thought Prompts

Some benefits of the chain-of-thought method are as follows:

- Improved Accuracy – By breaking down a problem into smaller, manageable steps, the model is less likely to make errors.

- Enhanced Clarity –It provides clear reasoning paths, making the model's thought process more transparent and understandable.

- Better Handling of Complexity – It allows the model to tackle more complex tasks by dealing with one step at a time.

- Versatility – The chain-of-thought technique can be applied to various domains, including math, logic, and even some types of creative writing where logical sequencing is important.

- Structured Output – The model's output is more structured and methodical, reflecting a clear line of reasoning.

13.2 The "before-after-bridge" technique

Description

- This is a technique where you first describe the current situation or challenge ("Before").

- You next describe your goal or desired outcome, highlighting key goals, requirements and constraints ("After").

- You then ask the model to provide you with a step-by-step process for getting from your current state to where you want to be.

Example #1 – Retirement planning

- Before: I'm 40 years old and unprepared for retirement, meaning I only have a small amount in saving and minimal investments.

- After: I want to comfortably retire by age 65, with enough savings to support my desired lifestyle and any potential healthcare needs.

- Bridge: Provide a detailed, step-by-step plan to build my retirement savings, including milestones, investment strategies and ideas. Also, consider money-saving tax strategies.

Example #2 – A corporate restructuring step plan

- Before: Parent Entity X currently owns Subsidiary Y, which operates as an integrated part of Parent Entity X's business.

- After: The goal is to spin off Subsidiary Y as a fully independent business entity. Post-spin-off, both Entity X and Subsidiary Y will be owned by the original shareholders of Entity X.

- Bridge: Provide a step-by-step plan for completing this spin-off, covering each major phase in detail. For each step, address the operational, legal, regulatory, accounting, tax, and treasury considerations involved in spinning off Subsidiary Y as an independent entity.

- In your output, include specific tasks and any necessary documentation, regulatory filings, and key transition activities. Ensure the plan is efficient but thorough, with essential steps for a compliant and smooth transition.[15]

13.3 The "few-shot" prompt

Description

A "few-shot prompt"[16] is a technique where you:

- Tell ChatGPT what you want it to do.
- Provide two to five few examples to show the model the specific style, format, or type of information you want in the response.
- Give the model the actual task you want it to perform.

By including examples of what you want, you will help ChatGPT to better understand and follow the structure and tone you prefer, resulting in more accurate, relevant, and usable responses.[17]

Scenario

- Assume you want ChatGPT to draft tax explanations for clients or non-tax colleagues in plain language.

- Instead of asking the model to "explain Section 179 deductions," you can improve the output by providing a few examples of how you'd like these explanations to look.

---

[15] Many step plans have similar steps. You can use one or more existing step plans to train ChatGPT on creating a new step plan.

[16] The name "few-shot prompt" comes from the field of machine learning, specifically from training techniques in natural language processing.

[17] The few-shot prompt method is a good approach to follow when creating custom GPTs.

- In reviewing and processing the examples you provide, ChatGPT will use the same straightforward format and language, making your response more predictable and aligned with your needs and expectations.

Sample CPA-related few-shot prompt

Explain complex tax concepts for my non-tax business colleagues in plain language. Use the following style and examples as a guide:

> Example 1: Depreciation
> Depreciation spreads out the cost of a large purchase over its useful life. Thus, if your business buys equipment that will last for ten years, you must deduct part of that cost each year for ten years rather than all at once.
>
> Example 2: Transfer Pricing
> Transfer pricing refers to setting the prices for transactions between a company's subsidiaries in different countries. It's a key factor in international tax planning and must comply with tax regulations in each country to avoid penalties. Transfer pricing can impact a company's taxable income in each location, making proper documentation essential.

Now, explain Section 263A in the same format and style.

13.4 A scenario-based prompt

Description

- Use this technique to present a hypothetical scenario, often with a complex set of circumstances, and ask the model to analyze possible outcomes and recommend an approach.

- This is useful for strategic decision-making, such as financial planning under different economic conditions.

Sample prompt

- Imagine a scenario where a company's business income has dropped by 20% during the quarter.

- Describe the potential impacts on operations and suggest at least three strategies to manage cash flow effectively in this situation.

- For completeness, list any strategies you considered but did not recommend, and why you did not recommend them.

13.5 The Outcome-Constraint Research Prompt (OCRP)

Description

- Use the OCRP technique when you know the outcome you want, but you're operating under real-world constraints such as time, budget, staffing, systems, or regulatory limits.

- Instead of asking ChatGPT for abstract ideas, you anchor the request in practical reality and force the analysis to focus on approaches that can actually work within those limits.

- This is especially useful for CPAs dealing with planning, process improvement, system changes, or compliance challenges.

How it works

1) Clearly state the outcome you're trying to achieve.

2) List the constraints you're operating under.

3) Ask ChatGPT to research or explain how similar outcomes are achieved in practice, given those constraints.

Key point: This framework shifts ChatGPT from brainstorming mode into applied research mode.

Sample prompt

I want to reduce our monthly close process from 10 days to 5 days.

Constraints:

- No additional headcount
- Must use our existing ERP system
- Minimal budget for new software

Based on these constraints, how do companies typically achieve this outcome?

- What approaches are most effective, and why?
- What approaches are commonly suggested but don't work well under these constraints, and why?

<u>Why this works</u>

- The OCRP approach filters out unrealistic recommendations.

- It can surface best practices that fit your actual environment (or at least get you going in the right direction).

- It helps you avoid spending time on ideas that sound good but won't survive implementation.

- This prompt structure is particularly effective when you're trying to move from theory to execution without overcomplicating the solution.

14 Adopt a Productivity-Driven Technological Mindset

14.1 The challenge for CPAs to keep up with AI

Up to this point, I've primarily focused on the technical aspects of using ChatGPT to generate answers to accounting, tax, and related questions. But what about the many other AI that are available, with more being introduced all the time? How can we as busy CPAs possibly keep up? The purpose of this section is to offer methods, strategies, and mindsets for staying on top of technology (vs. letting technology get on top of you!).

14.2 Recognize that core CPA work products stay the same

One way to stay grounded in the face of fast-changing technology is to remember that CPA-related work products have remained stable over a long period of time, and that trend is likely to continue well into the future. Here are examples of core deliverables that fall into that category:

- 10-Ks and financial statements
- Tax returns
- Tax provisions
- Technical memos
- Budgets
- Projections
- Workbooks supporting these and other accounting, tax, and financial calculations

Yes, it's true that we must evolve in *how* we complete these work products (that's always been the case), but the types of deliverables we produce haven't fundamentally changed in decades.

14.3 Keep the focus on productivity rather than technology

- For CPAs, I define productivity as completing high-quality accounting, tax and finance deliverables accurately and on time.
- Technology is NOT productivity. In other words, technology does not, by itself, produce anything.

- Thus, technology, whether in the form of AI or some other software tool, is only an enabler or accelerant of productivity.[18]

In summary, the goal for us as CPAs isn't to be the best at technology. The goal is to finish high-quality work products accurately and on time. Adopting that mentality makes it much easier to cut through the clutter and focus on technologies that matter.[19]

14.4 Adopt an investment mentality with technology

"Your scientists were so preoccupied with whether or not they could, they didn't stop to think if they should." – Dr. Ian Malcolm in Jurassic Park

- Adopting a mindset of seeing AI (and other technology) as a means to an end and not an end unto itself enables you to view technology as an investment.
- Consider the following example:

  o A work product currently takes 10 units of time to complete.
  o Will investing time, money, and effort in technology materially reduce the time required to complete the work product?
  o Will this be a one-time or a recurring improvement in productivity?

Asking and answering these types of questions will improve your technology-related decision-making and result in higher productivity instead of getting bogged down in needless complexity that doesn't matter.

14.5 Define what you want to accomplish

- Related to the previous point, defining precisely what you want to accomplish will help you to keep productivity (vs. technology) at the forefront.

- After determining your objective, consider if you can quickly and effectively complete your task with the technology and personnel *already available to you*.

- If so, it's not necessary to waste any more time or energy; simply focus on completing the project.

---

[18] This is consistent with Jim Collins's findings and commentary in his book "Good to Great."

[19] Another key finding from "Good to Great" is that high-performing organizations were NOT the best in all categories of technology. Rather, they were the best at *targeted technologies* that focused on key drivers of their business model.

- If, however, parts of the project are particularly manual, repetitive, or labor-intensive, consider technological solutions that could accelerate the work.

KEY POINT – Don't *start* with technology and wonder how it might apply to your work. Instead, *first* define what you're trying to accomplish and *then* determine if technology can make the process more efficient.

15 Professional Education Resources and Consulting

- Go to my home page at https://nctaxdirector.com and sign up for my mailing list to be notified of professional education updates.
- Contact me directly to arrange for onsite training on technology and productivity through a state CPA society.
- I also offer consulting services based on easy, flexible terms (refer to the web address above).

16 APPENDIX – What Changed in the 2026 Edition

16.1 Major structural expansion and re-organization

- Added a dedicated chapter on selecting the right reasoning/model level for CPA work (Regular vs Medium vs Advanced), instead of relying primarily on model-specific labels.

- Added a new chapter of advanced prompt templates designed for CPA work products (PDF review, messy spreadsheets, memo drafting, reconciliations, checklists, control/risk flagging).

- Added a new chapter of quick, high-impact prompt-engineering techniques that are meant to be used "in the flow of work," not as long "super prompts."

- Significantly expanded and restructured the Use Cases chapter (more use cases, more CPA-relevant ones, more operational detail).

- Consolidated and repositioned the productivity / mindset / keeping up with AI material into a later chapter and also pulled key "focus on one platform" guidance earlier.

16.2 Plan selection, privacy, and CPA-specific governance updates

- Updated the recommended subscription approach for CPAs from Plus-centric guidance to a Team-plan-centric approach (including solo CPAs) with clearer "why this matters" logic.

- Expanded/updated the confidentiality and data-handling discussion to reflect how the Team plan treats uploaded content and prompts (and why that matters for CPA workflows).

16.3 Model-selection guidance updates (how to choose "how much reasoning" you need)

- Replaced/de-emphasized model-name-based instructions (example: "use model X for deep reasoning") with a durable framework:
  - Regular for fast, low-stakes work
  - Medium for deeper reasoning when accuracy matters
  - Advanced for high-stakes, highly technical, or multi-step work

- Added guidance on managing usage/limits (so the model choice is tied to materiality and effort, not just curiosity).

- NOTE: The 2026 edition employs a "Regular / Medium / Advanced" naming convention to avoid model-name churn, but there are still places (example: memo-writing sections) that reference specific legacy model names in headings/labels. If you want maximum durability, those headings should be aligned with the tier naming convention.

16.4 Spreadsheet and data-analysis capability updates

- Updated spreadsheet guidance to reflect that ChatGPT can now read Excel files, while still recommending PDF conversion for dense, multi-tab, or complex workbooks where structure and cross-tabs can break analysis.

- Added more concrete "how to get reliable spreadsheet analysis" techniques (especially: provide specific workpapers, avoid "analyze everything," and control how the data is presented).

- Added a practical technique for Excel copy/paste: triple backticks to preserve formatting for formulas/tables.

- Added a new "intelligent data analysis" section explaining how to combine Alteryx (rule-based, auditable transformation) with ChatGPT (reasoning/pattern recognition)—including an example workflow for reducing large populations before applying AI reasoning.

16.5 Conversation management and long-term knowledge preservation updates

- Expanded chat management beyond "delete/archive" into organize + preserve:
  - Search chats for retrieval
  - Library as an image archive
  - Project Folders as the primary long-term organization system

- Added explicit guidance to avoid using "Archive" for important work and to use Projects instead (because archive is harder to access and not folder-based).

- Removed/de-emphasized older "manual archiving" approaches (example: saving key prompts in Word) in favor of native in-product organization.

16.6 "Get more from existing tools" expansion (Excel/Alteryx and beyond)

- Expanded the "use ChatGPT with tools you already use" chapter with a more explicit reverse-engineering workflow:
  - Explain inherited Excel formulas step-by-step
  - Explain Alteryx workflows tool-by-tool
  - Interpret tax software outputs/line items (example: deferred tax liability line items)

- Walk through ERP journal entries line-by-line

- Added more "prompt-ready" examples so the reader can use the technique immediately.

16.7 Use-case additions and updates (more CPA-relevant, more operational)

Added or expanded use cases including:

- Deep Search for research-heavy projects (with citation-style outputs and a more structured research workflow than generic "web search" prompting).

- Compare documents as a dedicated workflow (not just a passing mention inside PDF review).

- Analyze and summarize emails (extract asks, issues, action items, open questions).

-
- Review and complete complex forms, including a dedicated subset on tax forms (line-by-line interpretation, common omissions, schedule coordination).

- Review 10-Ks and financial statements using the same structured review approach used for returns/forms.

- Advanced text editing (editing/refining dense writing without rewriting everything manually).

- Transcribe handwritten notes into usable text.

- Language translation as a practical workflow for CPAs working cross-border.

- Troubleshooting technical issues (interpreting error messages, systematic debugging, configuration checks).

At the same time, the 2026 edition shifts attention away from some prior use cases that were less CPA-central (example: standalone emphasis on image-generation-for-presentations and the Merlin/YouTube-summary workflow) and reallocates that space to CPA work-product use cases.

16.8 Practical prompt-engineering technique additions (high-impact, reusable)

New "in-the-flow" techniques added and illustrated:

- Screenshots as inputs (faster prompting and less ambiguity for formulas, emails, workflows, and error messages).

- Top and Bottom Technique (delimiter method to separate your questions from pasted source text).

- Next Method (force one-at-a-time review of long lists and refine the output into a final consolidated list).

- Rolling review notes (maintain numbered notes across a review process without constant re-listing).

- Withhold expectations to test thoroughness (get an independent pass before steering the model).

- Incremental-input workflow for complex projects (upload source materials step-by-step; draft only when instructed).

- Start a new thread when performance degrades (structured method to migrate context and continue efficiently).

16.9 Advanced prompt-engineering updates (beyond the basics)

- Added the OCRP approach (Outcome–Constraint Research Prompt) as an additional advanced structure.

- Rebalanced advanced techniques toward methods that improve output quality on CPA deliverables, rather than "prompt theory" or external prompt-library-style approaches.

16.10 CPA example updates

- Updated the "tax updates" examples to reflect newer legislative framing (while preserving the same repeatable workflow for staying current on federal / SALT / accounting developments).